James Blunt

KU-052-752

Cockney rhyming slang for the good stuff.
Proof that one song is all you need.

Joined October 2009

87 Following   2M Followers

How To Be
A Complete and
Utter Blunt

Diary of a Reluctant Social Media Sensation

James Blunt

CONSTABLE

CONSTABLE

First published in Great Britain in 2020 by Constable

3 5 7 9 10 8 6 4

Copyright © James Blunt, 2020

The moral right of the author has been asserted.

All rights reserved.
No part of this publication may be reproduced, stored in a retrieval system,
or transmitted, in any form, or by any means, without the prior permission in writing of the
publisher, nor be otherwise circulated in any form of binding or cover other than that in
which it is published and without a similar condition including this condition being
imposed on the subsequent purchaser.

A CIP catalogue record for this book is available from the British Library.

ISBN: 978-0-34913-471-0 (hardback)

Typeset in Helvetica Neue by SX Composing DTP, Rayleigh, Essex
Printed and bound in Great Britain by Clays Ltd, Elcograf S.p.A

Papers used by Constable are from well-managed forests
and other responsible sources.

Constable
An imprint of
Little, Brown Book Group
Carmelite House
50 Victoria Embankment
London EC4Y 0DZ

An Hachette UK Company
www.hachette.co.uk

www.littlebrown.co.uk

Note: this is a selection of the best of James Blunt's tweets from 2009 to present day.
The timeline is not linear.

For Carrie Fisher

who taught me that words are even more powerful

than The Force.

Foreword

Twitter is awful – like a school noticeboard, where people are allowed to pin messages saying how much they don't like you. And although I tried ignoring the crowd of students gathered around each note, sniggering over their shoulders at me, it brought no satisfaction. So, I decided to post replies.

This has not been without its dangers. Should I cross some invisible but definitive line, they, the Twitterati, could, en masse, commit me to the ultimate purgatory – they could block me, or worse still, cancel me. But this is the world in which we live; where once we were told to keep our opinions to ourselves, with the invention of Twitter, everybody thinks their opinion should be heard. And opinions are like arseholes – everybody has one.

And so, it began – a journey of mutual humiliation. A journey into the depths of the gutter that is the human soul. To find out just how mean to each other we could be, and to justify it by the number of retweets and likes, and the size of crowd gathered to watch. Along the way, people have asked if I have a thick skin. I guess it stems from the fact that, if enough people tell you to go fuck yourself, eventually, you have to look in the mirror and work out whether they're right about something, or whether you choose to stand up and simply say, 'I'd fuck me'.

Then again, if there's no one left to fuck but yourself, what are you going to do? When celebrity fades, all that's left is the fight for relevance. And not until some brave soul, from the safety of his bedroom in his parents' house, with his trousers round his ankles, his proudest achievement being able to masturbate and tweet simultaneously, tweets that you are no longer relevant – only then will you know how I feel.

But through all of this, I still have hope. Once upon a time, my legacy was a three-minute, thirty-second pop song about some girl I'd seen on the underground. Instead, for a day in my lifetime, or maybe even two, I might be able to ascend the greatest of heights, to conquer the strongest of foes. Yes, if I get this right, I might just be able to do the unimaginable – to win the internet. And, in doing so, to have bestowed upon me the greatest of all prizes: to have men I've never met, nor wanted to meet, shake me by the hand, and say, over and over and over again, 'mate, I don't like your music, but I love your tweets'. This is what I'm fighting for. Right here, in the colosseum of our time, I am the gladiator, and you, the baying crowd.

Let's do this.

Dry **JANUARY** seems excessive. Dry Monday might work.

James Blunt @JamesBlunt

Big party. . . . Just woken up . . . and forgot to say . . . HAPPY NEW YEAR!

💬 53   🔁 113   ♡ 90   **3 Jan**

Ceej Tee @chickenoriental

I must be 1 of only 2 who genuinely likes every @jamesblunt song. The other person being him.

> **James Blunt** @JamesBlunt
>
> Nope, you're on your own.

💬 136   🔁 6K   ♡ 6K   **4 Jan**

Jos @dearjocelyn

James Blunt had his 15 min of fame and disappeared

> **James Blunt** ✔ @JamesBlunt
>
> Even less than that! The song was only 3 minutes and 30 seconds long.

💬 34   🔁 129   ♡ 147   **5 Jan**

M. Alif Novaldi @Alif_novaldi

Fuck you james blunt

> **James Blunt** ✔ @JamesBlunt
>
> I'm sorry, but you'll have to get to the back of the queue.

💬 54   🔁 721   ♡ 728   **6 Jan**

lauren @laurenlyal

Why does James Blunt sing like his willy is being stood on?

> **James Blunt** ✔ @JamesBlunt
>
> Damn thing's always getting caught under my feet.

💬 118   ⟲ 5.3K   ♡ 4.7K   **7 Jan**

James Blunt ✔ @JamesBlunt

Sorry I haven't put out new music for a while. Waiting till my balls drop.

💬 1.2k   ⟲ 5.9K   ♡ 64.6K   **8 Jan**

James Blunt ✔ @JamesBlunt

Maybe it's time I thought about making a new album?

💬 387   🔁 467   ♡ 367   **11 Jan**

---

katy_nicolson @katy_nicolson

Can we all take a moment and remember just how terrible James Blunt was

> **James Blunt** ✔ @JamesBlunt
>
> NO NEED. I HAVE A NEW ALBUM COMING SOON.

💬 182   🔁 2.7K   ♡ 1.1K   **14 Jan**

OliviaMae_98 @OliviaMae_98

James Blunt is my guilty pleasure 😍

> **James Blunt** ✓ @JamesBlunt
>
> Mine is anal.

💬 625   🔁 17.2K   ♡ 18.2K   **17 Jan**

Sarah @soz71

James Blunt could give me £1000 and I still wouldn't like him

> **James Blunt** ✓ @JamesBlunt
>
> OK I'll just take the £20 rubdown with happy ending then, please.

💬 103   🔁 697   ♡ 4.1K   **19 Jan**

shaklemore @shaklemore

@JamesBlunt how do you get a girl with your music

> **James Blunt** ✓ @JamesBlunt
>
> Wet.

💬 1.4K   🔁 18.3K   ♡ 123.1K   **20 Jan**

James Blunt ✔ @JamesBlunt

Click here for my upcoming tour dates: http://www.jamesblunt.com/tour

---

Scott Jones @ScottJonesy

I'd rather shit in my hands and clap

James Blunt ✔ @JamesBlunt

You're the first person I've met who's into that.

💬 250   🔁 1.4K   ♡ 12.9K   **21 Jan**

PhoebeChristaki @PhoebeChristaki

James Blunt's face fully aggravates me.

> **James Blunt** ✔ @JamesBlunt
>
> Then sit on something else.

♡ 100   ⇄ 4.4K   ♡ 9.3K   **23 Jan**

Alistair Spencer @spenno44

@BBCRadio2 please please please please stop playing James blunt please . . . thank you

> **James Blunt** ✔ @JamesBlunt
>
> Dad? Is that you!?

♡ 106   ⇄ 1.4K   ♡ 32.3K   **24 Jan**

Burns Night

heatherhjordisX @heatherhjordisX

Why is james blunt not touring in scotland??????

> **James Blunt** ✔ @JamesBlunt
>
> The Scots have taste.

💬 64   🔁 1.7K   ♡ 3K   **25 Jan**

Stott leaving your mask... @TheRstott

Reply to this with a sketch of what you think James Blunt's penis looks like.

♡ 652   ⟲ 5K   ♡ 51.2K   **26 Jan**

FEBRUARY

is probably a
better month to
go dry anyway.
It's shorter.

garymoody65 @garymoody65

@JamesBlunt why you only got 200k followers?

> **James Blunt** ✓ @JamesBlunt
>
> Jesus only needed twelve.

💬 186   🔁 4.9K   ♡ 5K   **1 Feb**

Omar @DrakesWriter1

James Blunt is the type of person to search for his name on Twitter

> **James Blunt** ✓ @JamesBlunt
>
> Omar is the type of person who searches for his name on Twitter and doesn't find anything.

💬 533   🔁 7K   ♡ 60.9K   **2 Feb**

Thomas Davias @ThomasDavias

Hey @JamesBlunt what do I have to do to get a follow?

> **James Blunt** ✓ @JamesBlunt
>
> Show me your tits, Thomas.

💬 190   🔁 3.3K   ♡ 4.2K   **3 Feb**

'I am delighted that Eddie Redmayne won
[a Golden Globe for best actor], but we
can't just have a culture dominated by
Eddie Redmayne and James Blunt and their ilk.'
Chris Bryant (to the *Guardian*, 2015)

James Blunt ✔ @JamesBlunt

To help people at the bottom of
the tree join those near the top,
give them a ladder, not a bow and
arrow. @ChrisBryantMP

💬 278   🔁 1.3K   ♡ 2.2K   **7 Feb**

James Blunt ✔ @JamesBlunt

Opinions are like arseholes –
everybody has one.

💬 298   🔁 2.8K   ♡ 3.4K   **8 Feb**

For The Many @ForTheMany2020

It's TODAY. Get yourselves down to #LabourLive up in Haringey for an amazing day of music and politics!

> **James Blunt** ✔ @JamesBlunt
>
> Alternatively, jump in your Range Rover and come and see me playing tonight in Chelsea.

💬 216   🔁 606   ♡ 5.3K   **11 Feb**

Valentine's Day

James Blunt ✔ @JamesBlunt • Feb 14

Happy Christmas, Interflora.

💬 66   🔁 920   ♡ 1.9K   **14 Feb**

Mike Sole @mikesole

The things you do for love. Waiting for 10am to buy tickets for @JamesBlunt for my wife. Oh it beautiful, it's true.

> **James Blunt** ✓ @JamesBlunt
>
> I think you mean things you do for a blow job.

💬 264   🔁 9.2K   ♡ 26.5K   **15 Feb**

Jordan Hill @JordanSHill

What ever happened to James Blunt?

James Blunt ✔ @JamesBlunt

💬 472   🔁 71K   ♡ 12.4K   **16 Feb**

James Blunt ✓ @JamesBlunt

For Lent, I've given up music. There is a god.

💬 221   ⟲ 2K   ♡ 3.7K   **17 Feb**

Ed Sheeran ✓ @edsheeran

@JamesBlunt marry me?

> **James Blunt** ✓ @JamesBlunt
>
> These kind of requests need to go through management, please.

💬 180   ⟲ 2.2K   ♡ 3.6K   **18 Feb**

James Blunt ✔ @JamesBlunt

Dis where I get ma hoes.

💬 754   🔁 18.6K   ♡ 67.6K   **19 Feb**

My birthday

James Blunt @JamesBlunt

Happy Birthday to me. 27 years old… in Spice Girl years.

💬 350   🔁 1K   ♡ 4K   **22 Feb**

---

thorsodinsons @thorsodinsons

Why does James blunt exist?

> James Blunt @JamesBlunt
>
> Because we can't rely on you.

💬 68   🔁 822K   ♡ 970K   **25 Feb**

James Blunt @JamesBlunt

Wondering how best to draw attention to the fact that I've added an extra concert in Sydney on March 14th.

♡ 892   ⟲ 3.7K   ♡ 26K   **28 Feb**

BLUNT WORDS ON . . . TWITTER

Nigel Nimaro @nigelnimaro98

Man, why don't you ever reply to positive comments about you?

> **James Blunt** ✓ @JamesBlunt
>
> Because I can't find any.

♡ 351   ⟲ 1.3K   ♡ 19.8K

jake_kaaaayyyye @jake_kaaaayyyye

James blunt's twitter isn't run by him you fuckwits

James Blunt ✔ @JamesBlunt

Yeah, right. Justin Bieber runs it.

💬 97   🔁 1.7K   ♡ 2.7K

Christian Blackman @chrisdb94

If it wasn't for Twitter everyone would've forgot about @JamesBlunt tbh!

James Blunt ✔ @JamesBlunt

And the most relevant you'll ever be is that one time James Blunt tweeted you.

💬 317   🔁 5.5K   ♡ 23.3K

MARCH
of the
Penguins
really moved
me.

Bieber's birthday

James Blunt ✓ @JamesBlunt

Can't believe Justin Bieber's balls
dropped before mine.

💬 360   🔁 7.2K   ♡ 8.1K   **1 Mar**

Chris's birthday

Devang @bruiselee

Chris Martin is not the guy who sang that annoying "you're beautiful" song, right?

> **James Blunt** ✓ @JamesBlunt
>
> No, he's the guy who sang that annoying "Paradise" song.

💬 104   🔁 3.8K   ♡ 5.8K   **2 Mar**

Fun fact: I've just bumped into James Blunt at a Premier Inn in Telford. He was very nice, held the door open for me. We nodded and carried on with our recluse life as a Premier Inn user.

James Blunt @JamesBlunt

Regards from Lyon. France.

💬 117   🔁 302   ♡ 37.7K   **3 Mar**

Anna @Jels_X

James blunt looks like a serial murderer

> **James Blunt** ✔ @JamesBlunt
>
> I know where you live.

💬 72　　🔁 1.6K　　♡ 2.5K　　**4 Mar**

_tusekile @_tusekile

James blunt is one ugly mother fucker

> **James Blunt** ✔ @JamesBlunt
>
> And how's your modelling career going?

💬 170　　🔁 2.4K　　♡ 2.4K　　**5 Mar**

James Blunt @JamesBlunt

I'd fuck me.

💬 464   ⟲ 12.2K   ♡ 15.4K   **6 Mar**

Lew @lewisscoot

@JamesBlunt looks like my left testicle

> **James Blunt** ✔ @JamesBlunt
>
> Then you need to see a doctor.

💬 152   ⟲ 3.6K   ♡ 6K   **7 Mar**

Thicky's birthday

---

blackeyelined @blackeyelined

Who is a bigger twat: James Blunt or Robin Thicke?

> **James Blunt** ✓ @JamesBlunt
>
> Me! Me! Pick me!

💬 135   🔁 1.7K   ♡ 1.6K   **10 Mar**

James Blunt ✓ @JamesBlunt

Happy Steak and Blowjob Day.

💬 620   🔁 1.3K   ♡ 9.3K   **14 Mar**

James Blunt ✔ @JamesBlunt

I am Napoleon Dynamite!

💬 220   🔁 2.1K   ♡ 5.7K   **16 Mar**

Singer from
Maroon 5's birthday

MrMtthwG @MrMtthwG

I almost can't tell if it's James Blunt or Adam Levine anymore.

> **James Blunt** ✓ @JamesBlunt
> Adam's wearing the ribbed condom.

💬 52   🔁 880   ♡ 3.2K   **18 Mar**

Mother's Day

Charlie_1232 @Charlie_1232

James Blunt has a twitter, what would he even tweet about?

James Blunt @JamesBlunt

Boning your mum.

🗨 270   ↻ 7.7K   ♡ 8.7K   **22 Mar**

Dan McEvoy @DannyMcEvoy

I find @JamesBlunt a fucking cunt...

> **James Blunt** @JamesBlunt
>
> I can find my own, thanks.

♡ 173   ↻ 3K   ♡ 4.5K   **25 Mar**

---

mattyblackett @mattyblackett

does james blunt have a vagina?

> **James Blunt** @JamesBlunt
>
> If I did I would never go out.

♡ 133   ↻ 1.7K   ♡ 42.5K   **26 Mar**

Samantha Victor @Sam_SamV

James Blunt makes my ears bleed

James Blunt ✔ @JamesBlunt

Sorry. Wrong hole.

💬 965   🔁 22.4K   ♡ 19.1K   **27 Mar**

Jay of the Dead @zomboy666

I've got fucking James Blunt in my head. I suppose at least that means my day can't get any worse.

James Blunt ✔ @JamesBlunt

Unless I find your bum.

💬 298   🔁 12.6K   ♡ 28.5K   **28 Mar**

APRIL

Fools – the
lot of us.

James Blunt ✔ @JamesBlunt

ANNOUNCEMENT: In keeping
with other greats such as
Prince, J Lo and Diddy,
I announce that henceforth,
I am to be known only as J Blo.

💬 220　　🔁 2.5K　　♡ 5.5K　　　**1 Apr**

Easter Sunday

Jesus Isaac @gravedads

thought James Blunt died

> **James Blunt** ✔ @JamesBlunt
>
> I did, but you'll NEVER guess what happened on the
> third day!?

💬 124　　🔁 2.9K　　♡ 3.4K　　　**4 Apr**

MyNameIsKyle23 @MyNameIsKyle23

Does James Blunt only have that 1 song? Lol

> **James Blunt** ✔ @JamesBlunt
>
> Says the None-Hit Wonder.

💬 50   🔁 1.1K   ♡ 1.8K   **6 Apr**

Dave Mc @daveymac99

Haven't heard much out of James Blunt for a while. Good.

> **James Blunt** ✔ @JamesBlunt
>
> Better get your earplugs ready. I'm just finishing up a new album.

💬 23   🔁 103   ♡ 130   **7 Apr**

Emily @Waaaaaayitsemmy

My mother is fucking listening to James blunt and singing along to it at this time in the morning

> **James Blunt** ✔ @JamesBlunt
>
> Early morning shag?

💬 84   🔁 1.4K   ♡ 2.2K   **9 Apr**

---

tilds @_idkmatilda

has James blunt done anything other than that one song in his whole career

> **James Blunt** ✔ @JamesBlunt
>
> Just that and a few super models.

💬 170   🔁 6.9K   ♡ 10.8K   **10 Apr**

James Blunt ✔ @JamesBlunt

It's actually a much better picture if someone else takes it for you. #GoFuckYourSelfie

💬 115   🔁 1.7K   ♡ 33.1K   **11 Apr**

_DawsonDaniel @_DawsonDaniel

Who'd win in a fight: Leona Lewis or James Blunt?

> **James Blunt** ✔ @JamesBlunt
>
> Blunt by technical knockout coz Lewis keeps bleeding, she keeps, keeps bleeding.

💬 26   🔁 169   ♡ 173   **12 Apr**

jesusberyl @jesusberyl

New James Blunt song tomorrow fucking fuck my arse

> **James Blunt** ✔ @JamesBlunt
>
> That day has arrived. You better lube up.

💬 1.1K   🔁 17K   ♡ 133.4K   **13 Apr**

James Blunt ✔ @JamesBlunt

My album launch party is rocking.

💬 461   🔁 1.2K   ♡ 26.1K   **15 April**

ChrisPaJones @ChrisPaJones

Why does James Blunt have a new album and why would people want that?

James Blunt ✅ @JamesBlunt

I'm guessing you're a philosopher.

💬 39   🔁 385   ♡ 608   **16 Apr**

The Bear @IndianBear27

you never anser my tweets. Want to be friends?

James Blunt ✅ @JamesBlunt

No, I just want you to buy my album.

💬 80   🔁 670   ♡ 4.1K   **17 Apr**

Man With Beard @RyanHudson2009

Don't know if I can imagine much worse than James Blunt's new album

> **James Blunt** ✅ @JamesBlunt
>
> Kids these days have no imagination.

💬 57　　🔁 1.3K　　♡ 1.6K　　　　**18 Apr**

Hollie Shand @HollieShand

Oh god...who let James Blunt release another album?!

> **James Blunt** ✅ @JamesBlunt
>
> Your god can't hear you. He's listening to track 3.

💬 146　　🔁 2.9K　　♡ 3.1K　　　　**21 Apr**

Isabel Micu @IsabelMicu

Every girl needs a James Blunt

> **James Blunt** ✔ @JamesBlunt
>
> I thought every girl HAS a James Blunt?

💬 109   🔁 1.1K   ♡ 1.8K   **22 Apr**

James Billington @bilge1979

I'd like you to know I'm going to be having sex to your new album later.

> **James Blunt** ✔ @JamesBlunt
>
> Sex on your own is actually just called wanking.

💬 124   🔁 2.2K   ♡ 9.1K   **24 Apr**

J-Raw @thejrodman

Now I have James Blunt stuck in my head...

> **James Blunt** @JamesBlunt
>
> And my balls on your chin.

🗨 167   ↻ 4.7K   ♡ 4.8K   **25 Apr**

Anders Cain @KOGAXWOLF

I wanna go see James Blunt so I can call him a faggot and throw a soda at him

> **James Blunt** @JamesBlunt
>
> I'm on a US tour now. Tickets available online.

🗨 106   ↻ 1.5K   ♡ 32.4K   **26 Apr**

James Blunt ✔ @JamesBlunt

Proud to announce that I will be headlining at ShitFest this year.

💬 186   🔁 2.1K   ♡ 2.6K   **27 Apr**

BLUNT WORDS ON . . .
CORONAVIRUS

James Blunt ✔ @JamesBlunt

Singing "I saw your face in a crowded place" suddenly seems a little dated.

💬 1.6K   🔁 29.9K   ♡ 216.4K

'Once upon A Mind' reaches No.6 in the Amazon UK charts on 26 April 2020

James Blunt @JamesBlunt

I see lockdown hasn't improved your taste in music.

💬 244 🔁 897 ♡ 15.2K

James Blunt @JamesBlunt

During lockdown, while many other artists are doing mini-concerts from their homes,
I thought I'd do you all a favour and not.

💬 7.9K 🔁 63.9K ♡ 534.5K

Richard Cheese @porkandparty

As if isolation couldn't get any worse, @JamesBlunt just came on the radio

James Blunt ✔ @JamesBlunt

Worse must be realising you're too thick to change the station.

💬 2.3K   🔁 11.9K   ♡ 170.6K

James Blunt  @JamesBlunt

It's not the reason you were hoping for.

Trending in United Kingdom ⌄
Keep British
2,206 Tweets

Trending in United Kingdom ⌄
Helicopters
10.1K Tweets

Trending in United Kingdom ⌄
James Blunt

Trending in United Kingdom ⌄
Cauliflower
5,383 Tweets

♡ 433 ⟲ 1.1K ♡ 25.1K

BBC News (UK) ✔ @BBCNews

James Blunt to host hospital radio show "I was flown in to lower morale over the airwaves," he jokes about his show for 170 stations. www.bbc.com

James Blunt ✔ @JamesBlunt

So you catch Coronavirus and have to be hospitalised and while you're thinking can my life get any worse @JamesBlunt comes on the hospital radio. Perfect.

💬 999   ⟲ 14.6K   ♡ 55.4K

MAY

the force be
with you.

Matt Burns @RealMattBurns

Can't believe I'm saying this, but I'm really enjoying @JamesBlunt's new album. What is happening to me?!

James Blunt ✔ @JamesBlunt

It's called the menopause, Matt.

💬 296   🔁 2.2K   ♡ 38.3K   **1 May**

Harry Conventional @StaleyHja

Might fuck about and start being a guy that listens to @JamesBlunt

James Blunt ✔ @JamesBlunt

THE guy.

💬 127   🔁 391   🤍 11.5K   **2 May**

Rachelle Russell @scriptlover4

@JamesBlunt should I recommend your music to my friend's

James Blunt ✔ @JamesBlunt

Not if you want to keep them.

💬 287   🔁 8.1K   🤍 55.3K   **3 May**

James Blunt @JamesBlunt

May the 4th be with you, @carrieffisher

💬 129   🔁 1.2K   ♡ 10.4K   **4 May**

---

vivadasilvas @vivadasilvas

James Blunt.
What a twat he is.

> **James Blunt** @JamesBlunt
>
> Like Yoda you speak.

💬 17   🔁 183   ♡ 264   **5 May**

James Blunt ✔ @JamesBlunt

Feeling bad that I sold @MikePosner a dodgy pill in Ibiza last summer.

💬 104   🔁 5.9K   ♡ 13.2K   **6 May**

Luce @Itslucexx

I can't escape James blunt... first it's on in the car and now on repeat in the shop

> **James Blunt** ✔ @JamesBlunt
>
> Next he'll be stalking you on the internet.

💬 385   🔁 32.1K   ♡ 107.4K   **10 May**

Laura @dinolauz

Who the fuck invited James Blunt to the Invictus Games?

James Blunt ✓ @JamesBlunt

Prince Harry. By text. BOOM!

115   2.5K   9.5K   **13 May**

'You're Beautiful' was released on this day in the UK in 2005

James Blunt ✓ @JamesBlunt

Anyone want a signed set list of mine from 2006?

JAMES BLUNT – 9:30 CLUB – 12/3/06

YOU'RE BEAUTIFUL
YOU'RE BEAUTIFUL
YOU'RE BEAUTIFUL
YOU'RE BEAUTIFUL
YOU'RE BEAUTIFUL
YOU'RE BEAUTIFUL
~~YOU'RE BEAUTIFUL~~
YOU'RE BEAUTIFUL
YOU'RE BEAUTIFUL
YOU'RE BEAUTIFUL

YOU'RE BEAUTIFUL
ENTER SANDMAN
YOU'RE BEAUTIFUL

○ 1.9K   ⟲ 52.5K   ♡ 167.9K   **18 May**

Noah Kinsey @thenoahkinsey

On my bucket list, I want to sit James Blunt down and explain – line by line – why his song "You're Beautiful" fucking sucks.

> **James Blunt** ✔ @JamesBlunt
>
> And I'd like to sit you down and explain – dollar by dollar – why I don't care.

♡ 1.1K   ⟲ 31.9K   ♡ 62.1K   **19 May**

Olivia @broliviah

I just had to listen to "You're Beautiful" by James Blunt in the office bathroom and I feel like someone is fucking with me.

James Blunt ✔ @JamesBlunt

Silent "with".

💬 127K   ↻ 3.8K   ♡ 18.5K   **20 May**

iChob @ChobDux

I used Shazam to discover "You're Beautiful" by James Blunt

> **James Blunt** ✔ @JamesBlunt
>
> This is embarrassing on so many levels.

◯ 195   ⟲ 9K   ♡ 39.3K   **21 May**

Eurovision Song Contest Final

James Blunt ✔ @JamesBlunt

You know we'd win the Eurovision Song Contest if you just had the balls to enter me.

◯ 523   ⟲ 5.1K   ♡ 9.4K   **22 May**

ArunSam_ @ArumSam_

James Blunt sounds like he is singing with a hot potato in his mouth

James Blunt ✔ @JamesBlunt

It's a silver spoon, achlehhh.

💬 128   🔁 600   ♡ 6.9K   **24 May**

emmajanehaze @emmajanehaze_

If @JamesBlunt smiled at me on the subway I would shit my pants in pure excitment

> **James Blunt** ✓ @JamesBlunt
>
> Not sure that's what I was aiming for.

💬 38   🔁 669   ♡ 1.1K   **25 May**

James Blunt ✓ @JamesBlunt

Just played You're Beautiful to 50,000 men. This is what it must feel like to be in Oasis.

💬 0   🔁 102   ♡ 42   **26 May**

John Mayer ✔ @JohnMayer

If you're pretty, you're pretty; but the only way to be beautiful is to be loving. Otherwise, it's just "congratulations about your face."

> James Blunt ✔ @JamesBlunt
>
> Mate, I've covered this already.

💬 446   ↻ 25.1K   ♡ 133.9K   **27 May**

blue @MilyOlivia

Only two people call me beautiful. Thank you mum and James Blunt

> **James Blunt** ✔ @JamesBlunt
>
> I'M SO SORRY. I THOUGHT YOU WERE SOMEONE ELSE.

💬 24   🔁 241   ♡ 238   **28 May**

---

jasmineleonie @jasmineleonie

James Blunt voted more annoying than paper cuts hahaha

> **James Blunt** ✔ @JamesBlunt
>
> But still marginally more entertaining than your tweets.

💬 21   🔁 98   ♡ 163   **29 May**

Lloydy_78 @Lloydy_78

I'm having a bad weekend, some guy just asked me if I was James Blunt!?

> **James Blunt** ✔ @JamesBlunt
>
> Me too. And even worse, I realised I was!

💬 18   🔁 149   ♡ 205   **30 May**

Farrsigh @Farrsigh

There's a "best of" James Blunt? Really?

> **James Blunt** ✔ @JamesBlunt
>
> Yup, it's called "Greatest Hit".

💬 79   🔁 1K   ♡ 2.5K   **31 May**

In
JUNE
or on June?

demisfenty @demisfenty

@JamesBlunt MARRY ME

> **James Blunt** ✔ @JamesBlunt
>
> It depends. Are you rich?

💬 69   🔁 732   ♡ 1K   **1 June**

YeahSheBoujee @YeahSheBoujee

What happened to James Blunt?

> **James Blunt** ✔ @JamesBlunt
>
> I heard he'd died.

💬 27   🔁 88   ♡ 78   **2 June**

TheInfamousEnjai @ewanhendrie

I try to hate James blunt but I can't

> **James Blunt** ✔ @JamesBlunt
>
> You obviously went to one of those schools where everyone got a prize.

💬 44   🔁 1.2K   ♡ 1.7K   **3 June**

---

josh @COYS28

if you tweet me, I'll make whatever you say my yearbook quote

> **James Blunt** ✔ @JamesBlunt
>
> I suck cock for coke.

💬 346   🔁 9.1K   ♡ 24.3K   **4 June**

BPGOD @handses

everytime i see "james blake" i think he's james blunt ....

> **James Blunt** ✔ @JamesBlunt
>
> That's kind of like saying every time I eat cake I think it's cunt.

♡ 61   ⟲ 1.7K   ♡ 4.2K   **5 June**

Craig Johns @craig_johns

Im on the metro and drunk while listening to music, but I genuinely don't know how @JamesBlunt isn't regraded as the best musician in the planet. You're all asleep!

James Blunt ✓ @JamesBlunt

Kids – this is why we don't drink and tweet.

💬 182   🔁 867   ♡ 18.2K   **6 June**

twixchick @paulinaboncan

Little bit of james blunt never hurt anybody

> **James Blunt** ✅ @JamesBlunt
>
> Depends where I put it.

💬 84   🔁 6K   ♡ 10K   8 June

IAMOWOMIZZ @IAMOWOMIZZ

why wont you just follow me

> **James Blunt** ✅ @JamesBlunt
>
> You sound like the stranger my parents always warned me about.

💬 11   🔁 98   ♡ 133   9 June

Kay @ItsKmama

It's a James Blunt kind of night

> **James Blunt** @JamesBlunt
>
> Quite wet and disappointing?

💬 396   🔁 6.2K   ♡ 40.7K   **10 June**

---

peteasywheezy @peteasywheezy

Stop searching for your name every day, it's getting weird.

> **James Blunt** @JamesBlunt
>
> You're the one following a stranger . . .

💬 10   🔁 40   ♡ 93   **11 June**

Jamie Mc @trimjim90

James Blunt gets on my tits.

> **James Blunt** ✔ @JamesBlunt
>
> And finishes in your mouth.

💬 1K   🔁 21.5K   ♡ 18.1K   **12 June**

---

iabiroy @iabiroy

James Blunt makes me sick

> **James Blunt** ✔ @JamesBlunt
>
> Then don't eat me.

💬 29   🔁 147   ♡ 197   **13 June**

joanna coles ✓ @JoannaColes

@JamesBlunt you're dead to me now, replaced by @edsheeran – a fellow Yorkshire!

> **James Blunt** ✓ @JamesBlunt
>
> He's from Ipswich.

💬 64　　🔁 734　　♡ 2K　　　　**14 June**

JamesMLVC @JamesMLVC

James Blunt is a pathetic cunt #obviousrhymes

> **James Blunt** ✓ @JamesBlunt
>
> JamesMLVC smells a little bit of wee #notsoobviousrhyme

💬 8　　🔁 89　　♡ 135　　　　**15 June**

82

ADAMDEVINE @ADAMDEVINE

I hope James Blunt has a bad day.

> **James Blunt** ✔ @JamesBlunt
>
> Mine was beautiful. Daniel Powter's on the other hand...

💬 15   🔁 131   ♡ 298   **17 June**

James Arthur ✔ @JamesArthur23

Artists these days literally just do impressions of stuff that's gone before, no originality and kids act like it's pioneering shit, really grinds my gears man 🗿♂ I must be getting old.

> **James Blunt** ✔ @JamesBlunt
>
> Lucky the world still has you and me pushing the musical boundaries.

💬 334   🔁 2.7K   ♡ 41.1K   **18 June**

James Blunt ✔ @JamesBlunt

Sorry haven't Tweeted in a while. I Blocked myself by mistake.

💬 338   🔁 5K   ♡ 13.2K   **25 June**

AnIrishChap @jthundersrocks

@James Blunt I broke up with my girlfriend because she likes your music. She's obviously deaf.

> **James Blunt** ✓ @JamesBlunt
>
> If she was your girlfriend she was probably blind as well.

💬 263　　🔁 3.5K　　♡ 13.8K　　　　**26 June**

James Mennie @mennie_james

@JamesBlunt must have a sad life just searching his name on twitter & wait to reply 2 stuf

> **James Blunt** ✓ @JamesBlunt
>
> Just searched your name. Nothing.

💬 26　　🔁 928　　♡ 1.3K　　　　**27 June**

Buizel0418 @Buizel0418

My mom hates James Blunt. xD

> **James Blunt** ✔ @JamesBlunt
>
> Because I won't pay the child support?

💬 172　　🔁 4.9K　　♡ 6.1K　　**28 June**

BLUNT WORDS . . .
IN THE CLASSROOM

Chance The Rapper ✔ @chancetherapper

Remember James Blunt?
YOUR BEAUTIFOOOE

> **James Blunt** ✔ @JamesBlunt
>
> You're.

○ 635 ⟲ 20.3K ♡ 134.5K

PAUL @Paulmurtha

@JamesBlunt Your an ignorant CUNT!

> **James Blunt** ✔ @JamesBlunt
>
> That moment you realise you've made a spelling mistake while calling me ignorant.

💬 236   🔁 2.2K   ♡ 4.3K

Kym @McKym

James blunt is a cunt.

> **James Blunt** ✔ @JamesBlunt
>
> I foresee a career in poetry.

💬 244   🔁 9.9K   ♡ 10.1K

_saraaaah10 @_saraaaah10

james blunt is a fucking pussy

James Blunt ✔ @JamesBlunt

I'm guessing that "a" was a mis-type?

💬 87   🔁 1.6K   🤍 1.7K

Lizzie akers @lizziea1

I want to kick James Blunt . . . repeatedly . . . I dont know why

James Blunt ✔ @JamesBlunt

Easy spelling mistake as K and L are right beside each other.

💬 56   🔁 1.9K   🤍 2K

Don't die in

JULY.

Peeps on hols.

James Blunt @JamesBlunt

I love my fan.

💬 1.2K   ⟲ 2.9K   ♡ 69K   **1 July**

Dave Briscoe @tobytyke69

15 years ago I hated @JamesBlunt for that song. Tonight it was one of the best gigs I have ever been to and that's a lot. Absolutely blown away.

> **James Blunt** ✅ @JamesBlunt
>
> Welcome to middle age, Dave.

💬 73   🔁 392   ♡ 10.9K   **2 July**

Joshua Willcox @joshwillcox69

think I enjoyed @JamesBlunt tonight more than the missus

> **James Blunt** ✔ @JamesBlunt
>
> I'm a bit tighter.

♡ 598   ⊔ 3.4K   ♡ 40.9K   **3 July**

Thomssmn @Thomssmn

Just realized how short James Blunt is !!!

> **James Blunt** ✔ @JamesBlunt
>
> It's only halfway in.

♡ 142   ⊔ 3.8K   ♡ 5.8K   **4 July**

David Carpin @DavidCarpin

The things we do for love. Sat through a James Blunt concert in Manchester yesterday as he screeched at my wife.

James Blunt ✔ @JamesBlunt

A James Blunt mask and some lube would have saved you the trouble.

💬 431　　🔁 2K　　♡ 30K　　　　**5 July**

Casy @cascon11

Waiting for @JamesBlunt to get on stage #Afterlovetour

James Blunt ✅ @JamesBlunt

Running late. Sorry. I've got the shits.

💬 344   ↻ 2.7K   ♡ 25.2K   **9 July**

James Blunt ✔ @JamesBlunt

I get paid £00.0004499368 per stream. Beers are on me! Cheers @Spotify

💬 503   🔁 5.4K   ♡ 13.6K   **12 July**

Ed Sheeran ✔ @edsheeran

Happy to announce my opening act on my North American tour is @jamesblunt x

> **James Blunt** ✔ @JamesBlunt
>
> What? I thought you said North Korea.

💬 181   🔁 4.4K   ♡ 22.5K   **14 July**

Donald J. Trump ✔ @realDonaldTrump

WITCH HUNT!

> **James Blunt** ✔ @JamesBlunt
>
> JAMES BLUNT!

💬 934　　🔁 18.5K　　♡ 116.1K　　**16 July**

James Blunt ✔ @JamesBlunt

Just realised that not a single Victoria's Secret Model follows me. FML.

💬 303　　🔁 2.7K　　♡ 8.8K　　**18 July**

James Blunt ✔ @JamesBlunt

Struggling to finish off with my left hand.

💬 255　　🔁 1.7K　　♡ 2.3K　　**19 July**

James Blunt ✔ @JamesBlunt

If I was in a band, it would be called, "Limp Willy And The Disappointments"

💬 204　　🔁 1.5K　　♡ 2.8K　　**20 July**

James Blunt ✅ @JamesBlunt

Trying to settle an argument - who should play me in my forthcoming biopic?

Tom Cruise	**31.8%**
Alan Partridge	**68.2%**

61,673 votes · Final results

💬 825　　🔁 322　　♡ 2K　　**22 July**

Tanya @Tanya_McDaid

I cannot stand James blunt

> **James Blunt** ✅ @JamesBlunt
>
> Have a seat. I have that effect on people.

💬 112　　🔁 2.2K　　♡ 5.5K　　**26 July**

megyn idk @megyn_wbu

Why is my brother listening to James Blunt

> **James Blunt** ✓ @JamesBlunt
>
> Coming out is hard.

💬 64   🔁 5.6K   ♡ 10K   **28 July**

Bethany Byrne @BWillett87

Can't stand your music but your comebacks are second to none

> **James Blunt** ✓ @JamesBlunt
>
> Can't stand your face but thanks for the compliment.

💬 55   🔁 1.6K   ♡ 3.5K   **31 July**

I want your
AUGUST
steamed body.

James Blunt ✔ @JamesBlunt

Anyone know any good dogging sites in Ibiza?

💬 365   🔁 3.8K   ♡ 7.9K   **1 Aug**

Lewis Chappell @chappell_lewis

James Blunt is playing in the gym. This is unacceptable.

> **James Blunt** ✔ @JamesBlunt
>
> I'm not playing. This is a serious workout.

💬 72   🔁 2.9K   ♡ 4.4K   **2 Aug**

Stu Morris @stuey_morris

@JamesBlunt my sister just got married at reef villa, Sri Lanka and apparently they are staying in the same room as you did. What we wanna know, did you bang in that bed...could be their claim to fame!

James Blunt ✓ @JamesBlunt

Sadly not. I had a dodgy tummy that night and shat the bed. Do send them my regards.

💬 833   ↻ 11.1K   ♡ 84.7K   **3 Aug**

NME ✔ @NME

Noel Gallagher says songs about his own life would be 'more boring than James Blunt'

> **James Blunt** ✔ @JamesBlunt
>
> For once, I agree with him.

💬 88   🔁 1.2K   ♡ 2.6K   **5 Aug**

Annie_luvsmusic @Annie_luvsmusic

@JamesBlunt do you have any pictures nobody should see on your phone?

> **James Blunt** ✔ @JamesBlunt
>
> not yet but feel free to send some

💬 2   🔁 44   ♡ 104   **6 Aug**

Independent ✔ @IndyMusic

Noel Gallagher says he cannot live in a world where Ed Sheeran sells out Wembley Stadium

James Blunt ✔ @JamesBlunt

Time to legalise assisted dying.

💬 153   🔁 3.5K   ♡ 5.2K   **7 Aug**

Alexandre Carrot @HiAleca

@JamesBlunt favorite guitar?

James Blunt ✔ @JamesBlunt

Ukulele because it makes me look big.

💬 5   🔁 39   ♡ 66   **8 Aug**

tianpogiaf @tianpogiaf

People who think you're beautiful –

1. Your parents
2. James Blunt

> **James Blunt** ✔ @JamesBlunt
>
> Only I was drunk at the time.

💬 139　　🔁 5.7K　　♡ 5K　　　　**9 Aug**

Eric Zelina @ezelina1221

Is James Blunt still remotely relevant?

> **James Blunt** ✔ @JamesBlunt
>
> Not if you're discussing spatchcock chicken.

💬 10　　🔁 62　　♡ 78　　　　**10 Aug**

kaserace_ @kaserace_

Who the fuck is playing James blunt?

> **James Blunt** ✅ @JamesBlunt
>
> Tom Cruise.

💬 25   🔁 541   ♡ 879   **12 Aug**

MommyOfSonya @jamesmcflyfan

James, I am your biggest fan. Please follow me. Please. It would make my day

> **James Blunt** ✅ @JamesBlunt
>
> Sorry, but my last name is not spelt 'mcfly'

💬 26   🔁 182   ♡ 315   **13 Aug**

James Blunt @JamesBlunt

Am making a solo sex tape. Will leak it online shortly.

💬 404   🔁 3.8K   ♡ 5.2K   **14 Aug**

Chelsea_Goulden @Chelsea_Goulden

Just got in a taxi and You're Beautiful by James Blunt is playing. Why thank you kind sir

> **James Blunt** @JamesBlunt
>
> I was talking to the driver.

💬 32   🔁 2.3K   ♡ 3.7K   **16 Aug**

yanto1973 @yanto1973

That James Blunt song is utterly horrific, horrific.

James Blunt ✓ @JamesBlunt

Yet so many people bought it, bought it.

💬 101 🔁 2.6K ♡ 4.4K **18 Aug**

---

limitle_ss @limitle_ss

Does James blunt still exist?

James Blunt ✓ @JamesBlunt

Only in places you can't get in to.

💬 85 🔁 575 ♡ 4.5K **21 Aug**

Simon Brotherton @AltySi

I cannot put into words how much I hate James Blunt

> **James Blunt** ✔ @JamesBlunt
>
> Try singing it.

💬 126   🔁 1.8K   ♡ 1.9K   **23 Aug**

Who? @something_robot

Waking up with James Blunt stuck in your head. Nowt worse.

> **James Blunt** ✔ @JamesBlunt
>
> Worse for me as there's nothing else in here.

💬 74   🔁 1.8K   ♡ 3.3K   **25 Aug**

James Blunt ✔ @JamesBlunt

WARNING if you see an email saying, "2 free tickets to James Blunt", DO NOT open it. It contains 2 free tickets to James Blunt.

💬 61　　🔁 174　　♡ 79　　　　**26 Aug**

Ariel @ArielEarevalo

Who remembers james blunt

> **James Blunt** ✔ @JamesBlunt
>
> Only The Beautiful.

💬 175　　🔁 3.9K　　♡ 12.6K　　　　**27 Aug**

Hannah Norman @HanMNorman

I've never fully understood why James Blunt felt the need to strip in his music video

> **James Blunt** ✔ @JamesBlunt
>
> You would if yours was this big.

💬 48 🔁 2.3K ♡ 3.8K **30 Aug**

BLUNT WORDS . . . FROM THE ARCHIVE

Ed Sheeran ✔ @edsheeran

my urban music award from 2011 turned up today...

> **James Blunt** ✔ @JamesBlunt
>
> My NME Award for Worst Album 2006 still hasn't arrived!

💬 17   🔁 180   ♡ 290

James Blunt ✓ @JamesBlunt

On this week, 10 years ago, your music taste sucked ass.

Pos	LW	Title, Artist		Peak Pos	WoC	Chart Facts
1	3 ↑	**YOU'RE BEAUTIFUL** JAMES BLUNT	ATLANTIC	1	7	⊕
2	1 ↓	**GHETTO GOSPEL** 2PAC FT ELTON JOHN	INTERSCOPE	1	4	⊕
3	2 ↓	**WE BELONG TOGETHER** MARIAH CAREY	DEF JAM/ISLAND	2	2	⊕
4	New	**ELECTRICITY** ELTON JOHN	ROCKET	4	1	⊕
5	4 ↓	**CRAZY CHICK** CHARLOTTE CHURCH	SONY BMG	2	3	⊕
6	5 ↓	**SINCE U BEEN GONE** KELLY CLARKSON	RCA	5	2	⊕
7	7	**ROC YA BODY (MIC CHECK 1 2)** MVP	POSITIVA	5	4	⊕
8	6 ↓	**AXEL F** CRAZY FROG	GUSTO	1	8	⊕
9	New	**NASTY GIRL** INAYA DAY	ALL AROUND THE WORLD	9	1	⊕
10	9 ↓	**SHOT YOU DOWN** AUDIO BULLYS FT NANCY SINATRA	SOURCE	3	8	⊕

💬 471   🔁 6.9K   ♡ 12.1K

James Blunt ✓ @JamesBlunt

If you thought 2016 was bad – I'm releasing an album in 2017.

💬 3.1K   🔁 144.8K   ♡ 275.7K

Jon Berry @jonberrywriter

On this day, we must all remember a collective tragedy from History. Eleven years ago today, James Blunt won an MTV Award.

James Blunt ✔ @JamesBlunt

Two, actually.

💬 90   🔁 777   ♡ 4.7K

Black Friday

Olly Murs ✔ @ollymurs

Fuck everyone get out of @Selfridges now gun shots!! I'm inside

Olly Murs ✔ @ollymurs

Really not sure what's happened! I'm in the back office... but people screaming and running towards exits!

Olly Murs ✔ @ollymurs

Evacuating store now!!! Fuck heart is pounding

Piers Morgan @piersmorgan

Stop tweeting mate @ollymurs. Nothing happened.

Olly Murs @ollymurs

Listen piers! I was shopping and then all of sudden the whole place went mad, I mean crazy people running & screaming towards exits. We found a small office to hide to which loads of staff and people were saying there was shots fired. If you was there you'd have understood mate.

Piers Morgan ✔ @piersmorgan

No. You listen, Olly. When you have millions of followers be very careful what you tweet. There were no shots, in fact nothing happened at all. So you stirred extra needless panic by tweeting false information.

> **James Blunt** ✔ @JamesBlunt
>
> From the man who published fake Iraqi torture pictures. LOL.

💬 998   🔁 19.3K   ♡ 85.6K

Zoe Wright @zoeintheskyyy

Who invited James Blunt to the royal wedding

> **James Blunt** ✔ @JamesBlunt
>
> I'll give you two guesses.

○ 397   ⟲ 4.4K   ♡ 33.4K

When
SEPTEMBER
comes.

Martín E. Rodríguez @supermarton

James Blunt es lo peor que le ha pasado a la humanidad desde Hitler

James Blunt ✔ @JamesBlunt

I'm guessing this is not good.

💬 283   🔁 9.9K   ♡ 15.2K   **1 Sept**

Amy @amymurrrray

When did James Blunt get funny

James Blunt ✔ @JamesBlunt

The moment I put out that song, I was knee deep in funny.

💬 41   🔁 860   ♡ 1.4K   **3 Sept**

Austin (Blackstar Plays) @Rockah12

Didn't know that @JamesBlunt was once a military guy. Can't imagine him doing soldier things. (no offense, James)

> **James Blunt** ✅ @JamesBlunt
>
> I look bigger with a gun.

🗨 112　　🔁 159　　♡ 2.4K　　**4 Sept**

ElliottAVFC @EliottAVFC

@JamesBlunt Fuck me I thought you was dead

> **James Blunt** ✅ @JamesBlunt
>
> That's never stopped you in the past.

🗨 66　　🔁 936　　♡ 1.5K　　**5 Sept**

Wakanda Shit Is That? @unemployedfatty

@JamesBlunt Are you gay? Just curious.

> **James Blunt** ✅ @JamesBlunt
>
> The latter.

💬 85　　🔁 2.1K　　♡ 4.8K　　**8 Sept**

---

anadinskywalker @anadinskywalker

my grandma just called james blunt a queer

> **James Blunt** ✅ @JamesBlunt
>
> Only coz I turned her down.

💬 129　　🔁 4.8K　　♡ 4.5K　　**9 Sept**

samanthamika @SamanthaMika

Does anyone else HATE james blunt's voice? I can't stand it.

> **James Blunt** ✔ @JamesBlunt
>
> I never liked the sound of my own voice. Till it made me rich.

💬 202　🔁 8K　♡ 5.9K　　**12 Sept**

James Blunt ✔ @JamesBlunt

It's not a selfie stick. It's a narcissistick.

💬 366　🔁 9.3K　♡ 11.2K　　**15 Sept**

James Blunt ✔ @JamesBlunt

Not even I think you're beautiful.

💬 1K   ⟲ 31.7K   ♡ 29.3K   **17 Sept**

Oktoberfest begins

jazz_mazz @jazz_mazz

James Blunt is ja auch eher so ein one trick pony oder?

> **James Blunt** ✔ @JamesBlunt
>
> Correct. I am indeed hung like a pony.

💬 127   ⟲ 1.6K   ♡ 2.2K   **18 Sept**

EugeneBarnardo @EugeneBarnardo

I love James Blunt as much as I love herpes.

> **James Blunt** ✔ @JamesBlunt
>
> I love that you're not ashamed to admit you have both.

💬 28   🔁 427   ♡ 524   **20 Sept**

James Blunt ✔ @JamesBlunt

Once we were besties.

💬 645   🔁 1.3K   ♡ 26.7K   **23 Sept**

James Blunt ✔ @JamesBlunt

My real name is James Blount, but I changed it as people teased me that it rhymed with 'count'.

💬 339   🔁 7.2K   ♡ 9.6K   **26 Sept**

James Blunt ✔ @JamesBlunt

I'm officially handing over my Cockney Rhyming title to @Jeremy_Hunt

💬 520   🔁 18.5K   ♡ 21.2K   **27 Sept**

James Blunt ✔ @JamesBlunt

Am changing my name to James Cucking Funt.

💬 457   🔁 2.8K   ♡ 4.4K   **28 Sept**

Lilley_padwar @Lilley_padwar

James Blunt rhymes with cunt, just saying.

> **James Blunt** ✓ @JamesBlunt
>
> Says Laura Lilley, whose last name rhymes with cock.

💬 94   🔁 1.5K   🤍 2.4K   **29 Sept**

James Blunt @JamesBlunt

I'm now making merchandise specifically for people who DON'T like my music...

💬 215   🔁 1K   ♡ 1.5K   **30 Sept**

Was
OCTOBER
a flop?

Atlantic Records UK ✔ @AtlanticRcrdsUK

@JamesBlunt's album #BackToBedlam is just £1.99 on @googleplay this week #ThrowbackThursday

James Blunt ✔ @JamesBlunt

What the fuck??

💬 309   🔁 5.4K   ♡ 12.5K   **1 Oct**

Dan Ryan @ThatDanRyan

Who the fuck is James Blunt?

> **James Blunt** ✅ @JamesBlunt
>
> I am the fuck James Blunt.

💬 671   🔁 3.6K   ♡ 54.5K   **2 Oct**

GenCassista @GenCassista

Does anyone still care about James Blunt?

> **James Blunt** ✅ @JamesBlunt
>
> Thanks for asking.

💬 112   🔁 1.3K   ♡ 2K   **3 Oct**

Bianca @Bajoena

@JamesBlunt not a really big fan, but was listening to your new album, and boy! Wow! I really love the "don't give me those eyes" song!

> **James Blunt** ✔ @JamesBlunt
>
> I don't really like you either, but I'm glad you like the song.

◯ 322   ⟲ 4.5K   ♡ 26.2K   **5 Oct**

teamtommo58 @teamtommo58

James blunt your music sucks #fact

> **James Blunt** ✓ @JamesBlunt
>
> As does your missus.

💬 440   🔁 8.5K   ♡ 7.1K   **8 Oct**

Shell Smith @xox_Shell_xox

Is there one single James Blunt fan out there?

> **James Blunt** ✓ @JamesBlunt
>
> Most of them are single.

💬 151   🔁 2.4K   ♡ 2.9K   **10 Oct**

AmirM96 @AmirM96

why have I got James Blunt stuck in my head this morning

> **James Blunt** ✔ @JamesBlunt
>
> My bad. Tea-bagging gone wrong.

💬 68   🔁 1.9K   ♡ 2.7K   **11 Oct**

AtaraMcBooth @AtaraMcBooth

Who the fuck is cheering for fucking James Blunt.

> **James Blunt** ✔ @JamesBlunt
>
> My mum's in the audience.

💬 40   🔁 798   ♡ 1K   **12 Oct**

Tim Bolton * @timbolton1

Bruce Springsteen on the show and yet we have to listen to music from James fucking Blunt. #GrahamNortonShow

> **James Blunt** ✔ @JamesBlunt
>
> You got what you deserved.

💬 596　　🔁 2K　　♡ 43.2K　　**13 Oct**

Dayoom_Q8 @Dayoom_Q8

@JamesBlunt sing me to sleep :$

> **James Blunt** ✔ @JamesBlunt
>
> Do I have to? I'm more of a finish & roll over kinda guy.

💬 130　　🔁 3.2K　　♡ 3.9K　　**14 Oct**

AlastairBroon @AlastairBroon

Every time that James Blunt opens his mouth I'd like to punch him in it

> **James Blunt** ✓ @JamesBlunt
>
> Glad you're not my dentist.

💬 83   🔁 2.1K   ♡ 2.4K   **16 Oct**

Rob Makin @RobMakin

James Blunt's back with a new single! This may be the worst thing that's happened in my life.

> **James Blunt** ✓ @JamesBlunt
>
> Good sense of perspective there.

💬 20   🔁 298   ♡ 449   **18 Oct**

Sha Sha's Bae @Jus_N1c

Does James Blunt still make music?

> **James Blunt** ✓ @JamesBlunt
>
> No. Just noise.

💬 292   🔁 3.4K   ♡ 22.5K   **19 Oct**

Joe Crown @joe__crown

2 bullets, one gun, James Blunt and Noel Edmunds. Without doubt

> **James Blunt** ✓ @JamesBlunt
>
> I preferred "2 girls, 1 cup", but whatever you're into.

💬 82   🔁 3.5K   ♡ 3.2K   **20 Oct**

CameronHood95 @CameronHood95

Fucking James blunt

> **James Blunt** ✔ @JamesBlunt
>
> What would you like to be doing right now?

💬 86   🔁 1.3K   ♡ 1.7K   **21 Oct**

Mig Weston @MigsterMMA

Jesus christ, James Blunt's got a new album out. Is there anything else that can go wrong?

> **James Blunt** ✔ @JamesBlunt
>
> Yes. He could start tweeting you.

💬 137   🔁 3.7K   ♡ 2.8K   **22 Oct**

Trah @TroyJosephDavis

no one really likes James Blunt right?

> **James Blunt** ✔ @JamesBlunt
>
> Yeah, I bought those 20 million albums myself.

💬 209   🔁 7K   ♡ 10.5K   **23 Oct**

KevPharmacist @KevPharmacist

Very tempted to start following James Blunt after his brilliant trolling. Then remembered: He's James Blunt.

> **James Blunt** ✔ @JamesBlunt
>
> Fair one.

💬 21   🔁 376   ♡ 675   **24 Oct**

James Blunt ✔ @JamesBlunt

I'd fuck me.

◯ 2.7K   ⇄ 2.4K   ♡ 52.5K   **25 Oct**

Paige Fergusson @paigefergg

Bloody hell why is James Blunt still going

James Blunt ✔ @JamesBlunt

Viagra and coffee mostly.

💬 108   🔁 3.5K   ♡ 4.1K   **27 Oct**

Katie @snapeinparis

james blunt really does creep me the fuck out

James Blunt ✔ @JamesBlunt

I followed you. Home.

💬 65   🔁 1.6K   ♡ 2.2K   **31 Oct**

BLUNT WORDS . . .
IN MEMORIAM

James Blunt @JamesBlunt

Sweet dreams, darling @carrieffisher. I'm gonna miss you. So much. X

♡ 85   ⟲ 1K   ♡ 8K

James Blunt ✔ @JamesBlunt

At the Q Awards years ago, when @NoelGallagher was saying he was leaving Ibiza because I'd moved there, and @DamonAlbarn refused to be in the same picture as me, and @PaulWellerHQ was saying he'd rather eat his own shit than work with me, Keith Flint came over, gave me a hug, and said how thrilled he was for my success.

Keith, I only met you once, but I shed a tear at the news of your death. In our business, there are no prizes for being kind, but if there was, that Grammy would be yours.

💬 1.1K   🔁 15.9K   ♡ 102.4K

Is M~~N~~OVEMBER
still a thing?

James Blunt @JamesBlunt

Slightly dismayed that the one time I'm on TV in the last 10 years is on a @LouisTheroux documentary about Jimmy Savile

♡ 247   ⇄ 10.3K   ♡ 33.5K   **1 Nov**

Free Follow @sassyfalahee

omfg james blunt is on the tv downstairs can this day get any worse!

> **James Blunt** ✔ @JamesBlunt
>
> Coming upstairs now.

💬 81   🔁 3K   ♡ 5.3K   **3 Nov**

James Blunt ✔ @JamesBlunt

Lots of people asking me what I've been up to recently. @FayeCarruthers

💬 894   🔁 6.3K   ♡ 53.8K   **4 Nov**

James Blunt ✔ @JamesBlunt

Must be approaching that time in my career when I do "I'm A Celebrity, Get Me Out Of Here."

💬 312   🔁 2.6K   ♡ 8.9K   **6 Nov**

Tony Langfield @tony_langfield

My first tweet, downloaded twitter just to message you this your bruce springsteen cover on radio 2. Think ive listened over 100times, outstanding doesnt cover it. Better than original. New fan.

James Blunt ✔ @JamesBlunt

Blocked.

💬 191   🔁 469   ♡ 11.4K   **7 Nov**

James Blunt ✔ @JamesBlunt

Good news for the UK:
I'm being deported to Australia.

Bad news for Australia:
I'm your new X Factor judge.

💬 362　　🔁 2.7K　　♡ 7.6K　　**8 Nov**

---

chris witt @chriswitt09

Watching an old Top Gear, with James Blunt on! He has the most irritating voice ever, and such a prick!!

> **James Blunt** ✔ @JamesBlunt
>
> Irritating voice but impressive cock. I'm happy with that.

💬 235　　🔁 6.8K　　♡ 18.1K　　**9 Nov**

Hinchy @dmhinchy

James Blunt is a major bell end

> **James Blunt** ✔ @JamesBlunt
>
> That's Captain Bell-End to you, Hinchy.

💬 91   🔁 1.4K   ♡ 1.7K   **11 Nov**

Liverpool Arena ✔ @EchoArena

Are you a massive @JamesBlunt fan? We want to hear your favourite track!

> **James Blunt** ✔ @JamesBlunt
>
> I doubt either of them will answer.

💬 88   🔁 486   ♡ 1.2K   **12 Nov**

va_va_vati @va_va_vati

I have this dire need to listen to James Blunt when I'm menstruating

> **James Blunt** ✓ @JamesBlunt
>
> Useful feedback. I'll pass this onto my marketing team.

💬 71   🔁 1.8K   ♡ 2.2K   **13 Nov**

KYLE @KyleB_96

James blunt – broken strings is a tune

> **James Blunt** ✓ @JamesBlunt
>
> A tune by James Morrison.

💬 53   🔁 1.1K   ♡ 2.6K   **16 Nov**

MiissAshley @MiissAshley

Nothing fucks your vibe up more than James Blunt coming on your Young Money Pandora 🔫

> **James Blunt** ✔ @JamesBlunt
>
> At least it's not on your face.

💬 93   🔁 3.6K   ♡ 4.9K   **17 Nov**

Mirror Celeb ✔ @MirrorCeleb

James Blunt 'heats up grub using his armpits' instead of using microwave

James Blunt ✔ @JamesBlunt

Because the @DailyMirror believes everything it reads in the @DailyStarUK.

💬 291   🔁 270   ♡ 5.6K   **21 Nov**

JimJimhawker @JimJimhawker

Have agreed to go and see james blunt with my mum. . . .

> **James Blunt** ✔ @JamesBlunt
>
> This is embarrassing on so many levels.

💬 65   🔁 1.3K   ♡ 2.8K   **22 Nov**

Bitch Mag ✔ @b1tchmag

Katie Hopkins branded a 'James Blunt' by critics after she slams overweight children

> **James Blunt** ✔ @JamesBlunt
>
> A career low for me.

💬 208   🔁 4.4K   ♡ 9.5K   **23 Nov**

Olivia Esposito @ooliviae

James Blunt is the rudest cunt on this earth, I fucking hate him

James Blunt ✔ @JamesBlunt

U're just a jealous runner-up in the Rudest Cunt Competition.

○ 112 ↪ 2.5K ♡ 5.4K **27 Nov**

Name cannot be blank @Raghallaigh

@JamesBlunt Holy cunting christ your music makes me want to cave my own skull in with a hammer!

> **James Blunt** ✔ @JamesBlunt
>
> Be my guest.

💬 103   🔁 1.6K   ♡ 2K   **28 Nov**

Party,

DECEMBER,

fiesta, forever.
Come on and
sing along.

Hettie Jones @hettjones

James Blunt just has an annoying face and a highly irritating voice

> **James Blunt** ✔ @JamesBlunt
>
> And no mortgage.

💬 694 🔁 11.5K ♡ 12.7K **4 Dec**

---

abby @iAreAbby

Whatever happens to James Blunt.

> **James Blunt** ✔ @JamesBlunt
>
> Stays in James Blunt.

💬 5 🔁 138K ♡ 199K **6 Dec**

Rachel Johnston @RachelJohnsto96

@JamesBlunt my dog could do better!!!!!

> **James Blunt** ✓ @JamesBlunt
>
> Then your dog should try harder.

💬 82　　🔁 1.5K　　♡ 2.1K　　　　**11 Dec**

James Blunt @JamesBlunt

Mariah Carey's gonna be pissed at this...

≡ ← ↻   **sky** bet   Join Log in

UK Christmas Number One 2019
UK Christmas Number One

UK Christmas Number One	^
James Blunt	4/1
Celebrity X Factor 2019 Winner	11/2
Adele	6/1
Ed Sheeran	6/1
Robbie Williams	6/1
WHAM	6/1
Arizona Zervas	13/2
Lewis Capaldi	7/1

💬 323   🔁 915   ♡ 16.5K   **13 Dec**

169

Nick @NickWoodley

How do you feel about James Blunt? I'd tag him in but I'm frightened of him on Twitter.

> **James Blunt** ✔ @JamesBlunt
>
> I'll find you anyway.

♡ 224   ⇄ 1.6K   ♡ 31.6K   **16 Dec**

Muzakir Ahmed @MuzakirAhmed

@JamesBlunt your music's shit

> **James Blunt** ✔ @JamesBlunt
>
> And it's taken you a decade to figure that out.

♡ 142   ⇄ 1.2K   ♡ 2.2K   **19 Dec**

kev @Khiggs3310

Why does James Blunt have a million followers? He stopped being relevant in 2009

> **James Blunt** ✓ @JamesBlunt
>
> 2006, actually.

💬 162   🔁 4.5K   ♡ 7.4K   **23 Dec**

James Blunt ✓ @JamesBlunt

Happy Birthday, Jesus.

💬 435   🔁 10.4K   ♡ 13.2K   **25 Dec**

James Blunt ✓ @JamesBlunt

To be honest, I don't even really like music.

💬 444   🔁 7.4K   ♡ 12.5K   **26 Dec**

1984 @Espinalx3

No worries at least James Blunt thinks you are beautiful.

> **James Blunt** ✓ @JamesBlunt
> I swear on my life, I don't.

💬 7   🔁 172   ♡ 180   **28 Dec**

Ambre @JonasKryptonite

why don't you tweet people that actually like you very very much?

> **James Blunt** ✔ @JamesBlunt
>
> That generation tend not to use Twitter.

○ 103   ⟲ 987   ♡ 4.6K   **30 Dec**

Sith Master Rodimus @Roddy77777

Oh look the posh c . . . backing Brexit who lives in Ibiza and has a Chantal in Switzerland has a new album out. Don't think any reminders will be buying it @JamesBlunt

> **James Blunt** ✔ @JamesBlunt
>
> Things that are true in this tweet: I am a posh cunt, I live in Ibiza, and I have a new album out.

💬 655   🔁 826   ♡ 15.6K   **31 Dec**

Last Words

I have learnt a great deal on this Twitter adventure. Primarily, that people confuse James Blake with James Blunt, which is the same three-letter mistake I made when I found myself shagging cake. But whilst others might correct their mistakes, I enjoyed mine. The cake felt good, and it was mine to eat afterwards. It has also left me with questions – like if you were having anal sex in a darkened room with Adam Levine and me, and Adam was wearing a ribbed condom, would you be able to tell who's who? It's something to think about. At times, it's left me with a bitter taste in my mouth – like the time I wrote to Jimmy Savile and he never wrote back. But more than anything, it has taught me perspective – I have stood on the edge of humanity, looked back and . . . farted.

It seems to me that Twitter brings out the worst in people but, like alcohol, it doesn't change us – it just reveals who we really are. And whilst I should probably be concerned that I come across as some kind of posh, perverted twat, Twitter doesn't have the feature to block myself. It's really up to you to do that.

But I'd be lying if I said this hasn't been fun. Where once I was being bullied by an entire nation, Twitter gave me a voice to reply with a simple 'up yours'. And if you were born with a name that rhymed with cunt, you'd have a barrel of replies up your sleeve too. Where once it was Grammy, MTV and Brit awards, the biggest selling album of the noughties and the most Googled name in 2005, I now receive King of Twitter awards from the defunct *Nuts* magazine for men, and that for me, ladies and gentlemen, is vindication.

And so, for anyone else determined to hurt themselves and others online, I offer this advice: don't tweet in the heat of the moment – wait till you don't care so much, because whoever cares the least has the power. And don't take yourself seriously because, if you do, the joke's on you. And don't make jokes about dropping the soap in the men's showers, even if you went to boarding school, because if you do, Stonewall will come for your ass.

Now wipe your bum and get back in there.

Acknowledgments

Thanks to my very understanding wife and God (@TheTweetOfGod), and to Prince Philip for writing my tweets.

Photo credits

P24 © Mark Surridge

P56 Isabel Infantes/PA Archive/PA Images

P117 Official Singles Chart Top 40

P130 Evan Agostini/Getty Images

P153 *Louis Theroux: Savile*, BBC Two,
   BBC Studios

P155 Andrew Lunn Photography/Shutterstock

P161 People Picture/Willi Schneider/Shutterstock